D0647088

11/16/16

Smokejumpers

by Meish Goldish

Consultant: Sarah E. Berns
Former Smokejumper, United States Forest Service

BEARPORT
PUBLISHING

New York, New York

Credits

Cover and Title Page, © Brad Wilson/Getty Images, © Kari Greer Photography, © Alin Brotea/Shutterstock, and © Paulo Manuel Furtado Pires/Thinkstock; 4–5, © Patrick Orton/Corbis; 6, © Mike McMillan/Spotfire Images; 7, © Northern California Geographic Area Coordination Center (ONCC); 8, © Peter J. Wilson/Shutterstock; 9, © Helen H. Richardson/Associated Press; 10, © Mike McMillan/Spotfire Images; 11, © Mike McMillan/Spotfire Images; 12, © Mike McMillan/Spotfire Images; 13, © Mike McMillan/Spotfire Images; 14, © Kari Greer Photography; 15T, © Charles Knowles/Shutterstock; 15B, © Kari Greer Photography; 16, © Mike McMillan/Spotfire Images; 17, © Mike McMillan/Spotfire Images; 18–19, © Mike McMillan/Spotfire Images; 19T, © Mike McMillan/Spotfire Images; 20, © Matt Mills McKnight; 21L, © Kari Greer Photography; 21R, © Justin Sullivan/Getty Images; 22, © Montanabw/Wikipedia Creative Commons; 23T, © Jason Savage/Alamy; 23B, © Public Domain; 24, © Zuma Press Inc./Alamy; 25, © Craig Allyn Rose/ San José Fire Department Photographer; 26L, © Ramona Hull; 26R, © Mike McMillan/ Spotfire Images; 27, © Mike McMillan/Spotfire Images; 28, © Kari Greer Photography; 29T, © Mike McMillan/Spotfire Images; 29BL, © Wacpan/Shutterstock; 29BC, © Tyler Panian/Shutterstock; 29BR, © Public Domain; 31, © ZUMA Press, Inc./Alamy.

Publisher: Kenn Goin
Editor: Jessica Rudolph
Creative Director: Spencer Brinker
Design: Emma Randall
Photo Researcher: Ruby Tuesday Books

Library of Congress Cataloging-in-Publication Data in process at time of publication (2014)

Library of Congress Control Number: 2013041504
ISBN-13: 978-1-62724-100-7

Copyright © 2014 Bearport Publishing Company, Inc. All rights reserved. No part of this publication may be reproduced in whole or in part, stored in any retrieval system, or transmitted in any form or by any means, electronic, mechanical, photocopying, recording, or otherwise, without written permission from the publisher.

For more information, write to Bearport Publishing Company, Inc., 45 West 21st Street, Suite 3B, New York, New York 10010. Printed in the United States of America.

10 9 8 7 6 5 4 3 2 1

Contents

Lightning Strike 4

Ready, Set, Jump! 6

Battling Wildfires 8

Racing the Flames 10

Rough Days 12

Lots of Help 14

Mopping Up 16

Having What It Takes 18

Parachute Training 20

Danger on the Job 22

Taking Cover 24

Why Be a Smokejumper? 26

Smokejumpers' Gear 28

Glossary 30

Bibliography 31

Read More 31

Learn More Online 31

Index 32

About the Author 32

Lightning Strike

It all started with a bolt of lightning on a summer afternoon in July 2012. The lightning struck a tree in a part of Montana's Lolo National Forest called Rattlesnake Wilderness. In an instant, the tree burst into flames like a giant match. The fire quickly spread to other trees. In no time, a **wildfire** covered the area.

A wildfire burning in a forest in Montana

Nearby, an airplane was on **fire patrol**. When the plane's pilot saw smoke rising from the forest, he immediately radioed fire officials on the ground. The wildfire was moving up a hill that had no roads. Officials knew that firefighters on the ground would have a hard time reaching the blaze. This was a job for smokejumpers!

Smokejumpers are firefighters who **parachute** from airplanes to reach wildfires. They often need to land in **remote** areas where there are no roads.

Ready, Set, Jump!

Eight smokejumpers at a **base** in Missoula, Montana, were sent out as the **first responders** to the wildfire. Their base was about ten miles (16 km) from the blaze. The firefighters quickly put on their padded jumpsuits, strapped on their parachutes, and boarded an airplane. When the plane was flying over the **jump spot**, the smokejumpers leapt out.

These smokejumpers landed near a wildfire in Alaska. Sometimes, smokejumpers land as close as 25 feet (7.6 m) from a fire!

Smokejumpers have bases in several western states, including California, Alaska, and Montana. These states are places where many wildfires occur during the summer months.

As the smokejumpers fell through the air, their parachutes opened. They guided themselves to the ground near the fire by tugging on their parachute straps, or toggles. The jumpers had to steer carefully. Why? One wrong move could cause them to be blown off course and into the flames.

A jumper who accidentally lands in a tree will tie a rope to a branch so that he or she can climb down to the ground. The jumper may have to climb more than 100 feet (30.5 m)!

Battling Wildfires

Wildfires like the one in Rattlesnake Wilderness spread very quickly. During hot summers with little rain, trees and grasses dry out. Wildfires burn this dry **vegetation** in a flash and then move on, hungry for more **fuel**. If there are high winds, flames will spread even faster.

Many wildfires are started by lightning or by people who accidentally start them when they build campfires.

Wildfires don't just destroy forests. They also threaten people who live near wooded areas. A fire may spread to towns and destroy homes and other property. Harmful smoke fills the air, making it dangerous to breathe. Smokejumpers keep all this in mind as they parachute down to battle a blaze.

 In 2012, Colorado had a very hot, dry summer. About a dozen wildfires burned more than 244,000 acres (98,743 hectares) and destroyed more than 600 homes. Thousands of people had to be **evacuated**.

During the summer of 2012, six people were killed in wildfires that spread across Colorado.

Racing the Flames

The eight smokejumpers who parachuted into Rattlesnake Wilderness needed to act quickly to **contain** the fire. After landing on the ground, they immediately started cutting a **firebreak**. Smokejumpers make this long, wide path by clearing away trees, grasses, and other vegetation. All that's left is dirt. When the wildfire reaches the firebreak, it has nothing to burn and it dies out.

Supplies, such as chain saws and shovels, are parachuted to smokejumpers after they land. This jumper is using a chain saw to cut down trees along a firebreak.

Sometimes, a wildfire moves too quickly for smokejumpers to make a firebreak. Instead, to stop the blaze, they create their own fire, called a **backfire**. To start one, jumpers use **fusees** or torches to burn the vegetation between themselves and the oncoming wildfire. When the wildfire reaches the burned-out path created by the backfire, it dies out.

This smokejumper uses a torch to start a backfire.

There are no water **hydrants** in remote forest areas. However, sometimes smokejumpers use hoses to pump and spray water from nearby lakes or rivers onto a wildfire.

Rough Days

Some wildfires are so huge that it can take weeks to contain them! Smokejumpers usually work 16-hour **shifts** in extremely hot conditions. According to smokejumper Rick Rataj, "You're in the heat of battle . . . so you don't really notice it's uncomfortable until you're done. Then you're like, wow, I'm all dirty and sweaty, and it's really hot."

Smokejumpers, like this one in Nevada, work long hours in areas that are hot and smoky.

At night, smokejumpers sleep on the ground. They have to deal with biting insects and **venomous** snakes crawling nearby. Sometimes, the jumpers work 14 days straight before they get any time off. After one day of rest, they return to battle the wildfire.

Smokejumpers eat mostly canned food while they're working.

A smokejumper from the base will drop food supplies by parachute down to the jumpers on the ground. The firefighters usually don't sit down for a meal until nighttime, when their shift is over.

Lots of Help

Smokejumpers are often the first firefighters to respond to wildfires, but they don't work alone. Sometimes, **tanker planes** fly overhead and drop sticky **fire-retardant** chemicals over a burning area. The chemicals keep the vegetation wet so it burns more slowly. Helicopters may also help out by carrying giant buckets of water to dump on the flames.

Chemicals dropped on a wildfire are brightly colored so pilots and smokejumpers can see exactly which areas have been sprayed.

If there are roads, teams of special firefighters called **hotshots** drive to the wildfire area to join the smokejumpers. Like the jumpers, hotshots work to contain the fire. Other firefighters may bring in bulldozers. The bulldozers quickly make firebreaks by plowing through grasses and shrubs.

After dumping water on a wildfire, helicopter pilots may refill their buckets at a nearby lake or river.

Hotshots often work in teams of 20 members to battle a wildfire.

Mopping Up

Even after a wildfire is contained, smokejumpers still have a lot of work to do. Once the fire dies out, they must "mop up" so the fire doesn't start again later. The jumpers slowly walk across every inch of burned ground, sometimes for miles. Along the way, they feel the ground for "hot spots." These are small areas where the fire may still be **smoldering**.

After a fire died out in Colorado, smokejumpers teamed up with a firetruck crew that had hoses. They sprayed the ground with water to make sure the wildfire didn't start again.

It took a few days for the eight smokejumpers in Rattlesnake Wilderness to put out the wildfire. The fire had burned an area about the size of two football fields.

Each hot spot needs to be put out completely. To do this, jumpers use their shovels to put dirt on top of any **embers** they find. After all the hot spots are **smothered**, the smokejumpers leave the area in a helicopter or through the forest on foot.

After containing a wildfire, these smokejumpers hiked out of a forest while carrying all their heavy equipment.

Having What It Takes

Making just one mistake while parachuting or fighting a fire can be deadly. As a result, smokejumpers have to be carefully trained. Smokejumper **trainees** are usually firefighters who already have several years of experience fighting wildfires. During training, jumpers are taught how different wind conditions can affect their parachute jumps. They also learn how to use their smokejumping equipment and how to **rappel** down trees with ropes.

Smokejumper trainees run to prepare themselves for the physical demands of their job.

Since firefighting is hard work, trainees have to pass tough **physical** tests. In one test, they must run 1.5 miles (2.4 km) in under 11 minutes. In the "pack-out" test, they have to hike 3 miles (4.8 km) while carrying 110 pounds (50 kg) of gear in 90 minutes or less!

Other physical tests require trainees to do 45 sit-ups and 25 push-ups in two minutes.

These trainees in Alaska are doing push-ups while it's snowing!

Parachute Training

Smokejumpers learn one more important skill during training—how to parachute from an airplane. At training camp, students drop from a three-story jump tower while wearing a body **harness** that is attached to a cable. This allows them to practice the correct way to exit, or jump out of, a plane. After they've learned how to do this, trainees take practice jumps with real parachutes.

A smokejumper must weigh between 120 and 200 pounds (54 to 91 kg). A lightweight jumper might get blown off course by the wind. A heavier jumper may land too hard and get injured.

These trainees drop from a 35-foot (10.7 m) jump tower.

Trainees also learn to steer their parachute so they land on the jump spot. However, this isn't so easy to do. In one of his first jumps to a fire, Rick Rataj accidentally landed in an 80-foot (24 m) tall pine tree. "I had to rappel down with all the guys laughing at me," he remembered.

During training jumps, smokejumpers land in trees on purpose in order to practice climbing down from them.

Smokejumpers make at least 15 practice jumps from an airplane before they are allowed to parachute to a wildfire.

Danger on the Job

Although smokejumpers are well trained, things can still go terribly wrong. One of the worst firefighting **tragedies** occurred in 1949. A group of smokejumpers from Missoula, Montana, parachuted into Helena National Forest to battle a wildfire in a **canyon** area called Mann Gulch.

Mann Gulch today

Smokejumpers first began battling wildfires in 1940, when two firefighters parachuted into Nez Perce National Forest in Idaho. Soon after, the **United States Forest Service** began to train many more smokejumpers.

As the smokejumpers went to work near the blaze, a strong wind suddenly blew the wildfire straight toward them. The jumpers tried to run away. Two firefighters managed to find shelter inside a crack in the canyon's rock wall. Sadly, 12 other smokejumpers were caught by the flames and died.

This statue at Mann Gulch honors the firefighters who lost their lives battling the blaze in 1949.

After the wildfire at Mann Gulch died out, forest officials inspected the area to learn how future tragedies could be prevented.

Taking Cover

After the Mann Gulch tragedy, the Forest Service developed a lightweight fire shelter to help protect firefighters from fast-moving flames blown in their direction. The shelter looks like a small tent and is made of materials that can withstand heat up to about 1,000°F (538°C). Firefighters who are trapped by flames can grab the folded shelter from their backpack and quickly open it up. Each firefighter takes cover inside one until the blaze passes over him or her.

A firefighter uses a fire shelter during a training exercise.

The shelters have saved hundreds of lives. In 1994, nine Colorado firefighters survived a wildfire when they took cover in their shelters. The firefighters had been dealing with difficult conditions as they battled the blaze, including high winds that caused the flames to spread 100 feet (30.5 m) per minute. Conditions were so deadly, however, that several other smokejumpers who used their shelters in the wildfire did not survive.

Firefighters taking cover in their shelters

A fire shelter protects a person in a wildfire for about two minutes before the tent burns up.

Why Be a Smokejumper?

A smokejumper has a very dangerous job. So why would anyone choose to become one? Just ask Ramona Hull, a smokejumper based in Idaho. A former college athlete, Ramona welcomes the physical challenge of firefighting. She also loves the thrill of the jump.

Ramona Hull traveling to a wildfire in an airplane

A smokejumper exiting a plane

Ramona recalled that her first practice jump "was really exciting, your heart is pumping." During her first actual fire jump, Ramona landed in a tree. She wasn't discouraged, however. She looked forward to each new jump. Thanks to brave individuals like Ramona, smokejumpers will continue to be the heroes who are first on the scene to battle deadly wildfires.

A smokejumper parachuting to a wildfire in Alaska

About 30 of the approximately 400 smokejumpers working in the United States are women.

Smokejumpers' Gear

Smokejumpers wear special gear during their parachute jumps. Here is some of their equipment.

A lightweight *helmet* protects the jumper's head when landing.

A *face mask* protects the face if the jumper lands in a tree.

A *reserve parachute* is used if the main one fails to open.

The padded *jumpsuit* protects the smokejumper from being hurt by tree branches and rocks when landing.

Leg pockets hold rope in case the jumper lands in a tree and needs to climb down.

Heavy *boots* protect the jumper's feet.

Smokejumpers wear special gear for protection as they battle wildfires. They also use many tools to dig firebreaks or set backfires.

A *hard hat* is made of strong plastic that will not easily melt in a fire.

A heat-resistant *jacket* prevents the smokejumper from getting overheated or burned by flames.

A *drip torch* is used to start a backfire.

A *fire pack* holds important equipment, including a folded fire shelter and a water canteen.

Gloves protect the hands from fire.

Fire-retardant *pants* protect a smokejumper's legs from getting burned.

A *chain saw* is used to cut down trees and saw logs in the path of a firebreak.

A *portable radio* keeps the smokejumper in touch with other firefighters.

A *Pulaski* is a combination ax and hoe. When making a firebreak, the ax is used to chop bushes and branches, and the hoe is used to loosen and dig dirt.

Glossary

backfire (BAK-fire) a fire started on purpose that clears an area of vegetation in order to stop an advancing wildfire

base (BAYSS) the place where a group of workers report for duty until they are called upon to do a job

canyon (KAN-yuhn) a deep, steep-walled valley carved out by a river

contain (kuhn-TAYN) to keep under control

embers (EM-burz) the hot, glowing remains of a fire

evacuated (i-VAK-yoo-*ayt*-id) moved away from an area that is dangerous

firebreak (FIRE-brayk) a path cleared around a wildfire to stop flames from spreading

fire patrol (FIRE puh-TROHL) the job of traveling around an area to check for wildfires

fire-retardant (*fire*-ri-TARD-uhnt) something that slows down the speed with which something burns

first responders (FURST ri-SPOND-urz) people, such as firefighters, whose job it is to be the first on the scene of an emergency to provide help

fuel (FYOO-uhl) something that is burned and is used as a source of energy, such as wood or coal

fusees (FYOOZ-ees) devices that create flames that are used to set fires or send signals

harness (HAR-niss) a set of straps worn by a smokejumper to connect him or her to a parachute or jump tower

hotshots (HOT-shots) teams of firefighters who reach wildfires from the ground and then work to contain the flames

hydrants (HYE-druhnts) large outdoor pipes connected to a water supply that are used in a fire emergency

jump spot (JUHMP SPOT) the area on the ground where parachute jumpers try to land

parachute (PAH-ruh-*shoot*) to jump out of a plane using a soft cloth attached to ropes to slow down the fall

physical (FIZ-uh-kuhl) having to do with the body

rappel (ruh-PEL) to climb down something by using a rope

remote (ri-MOHT) far from any settled place; hard to reach

shifts (SHIFTS) set periods of time in which a person works

smoldering (SMOHL-dur-ing) burning and smoking slowly with no flames

smothered (SMUHTH-urd) covered so that air cannot reach it

tanker planes (TANG-kur PLAYNZ) airplanes that drop chemicals on a wildfire in order to put it out

tragedies (TRAJ-uh-deez) terrible events that cause great sadness or suffering

trainees (tray-NEEZ) people who are being taught how to perform a certain kind of job

United States Forest Service (yoo-NYE-tid STAYTS FOR-ist SUR-viss) a government office in charge of protecting and maintaining forests in the United States

vegetation (*vej*-uh-TAY-shuhn) the plants that cover an area

venomous (VEN-uhm-uhss) able to attack with a poisonous bite

wildfire (WILDE-*fire*) a fire that spreads quickly over a large area, usually in the wilderness

Bibliography

Krauss, Erich. *Wall of Flame: The Heroic Battle to Save Southern California*. Hoboken, NJ: Wiley (2006).

Missoula Smokejumpers: www.fs.fed.us/fire/people/smokejumpers/missoula/

National Smokejumper Association: http://smokejumpers.com

Pyne, Stephen J. *Fire in America: A Cultural History of Wildland and Rural Fire (Cycle of Fire)*. Seattle, WA: University of Washington Press (1997).

Read More

Beyer, Mark. *Smokejumpers: Life Fighting Fires (Extreme Careers)*. New York: Rosen (2001).

Demarest, Chris L. *Smokejumpers One to Ten*. New York: Margaret K. McElderry Books (2002).

Landau, Elaine. *Smokejumpers*. Brookfield, CT: Millbrook Press (2002).

Tieck, Sarah. *Smoke Jumpers (Extreme Jobs)*. Edina, MN: ABDO (2012).

Learn More Online

To learn more about smokejumpers, visit
www.bearportpublishing.com/FireFight

Index

Alaska 6, 19, 27

backfire 11, 29

California 6
chain saw 10, 29
Colorado 9, 16, 25

firebreak 10–11, 15, 29
fire-retardant chemicals 14
fire shelter 24–25, 29
fusee 11

Helena National Forest 22
helicopters 14–15, 17
hotshots 15
Hull, Ramona 26–27

Idaho 22, 26

jump spot 6, 21
jumpsuit 6, 28

lightning 4, 8
Lolo National Forest 4

Mann Gulch 22–23, 24
Montana 4, 6, 22
mopping up 16–17

Nevada 12
Nez Perce National Forest 22

parachute 5, 6–7, 9, 10, 13,
    18, 20–21, 22, 26–27, 28
parachute training 20–21
physical training 18–19
Pulaski 29

Rataj, Rick 12, 21
Rattlesnake Wilderness 4, 8,
    10, 16

tanker planes 14
torch 11, 29
trainees 18–19, 20–21

United States Forest Service
    22, 24

About the Author

Meish Goldish has written more than 200 books for children.
His book *Disabled Dogs* was a Junior Library Guild Selection in 2013.
He lives in Brooklyn, New York.